KEEPING IN TOUCH

KEEPING IN TOUCH

NEW AND SELECTED POEMS

EUGENE MCNAMARA

Mosaic Press
Oakville, ON - Buffalo, NY

Canadian Cataloguing in Publication Data

McNamara, Eugene, 1930-
  Keeping in touch

Poems.
ISBN 0-88962-673-1

I. Title.

PS8575.N34K43 1998   C811'.54   C98-931170-8
PR9199.3.M36K43 1998

Published by MOSAIC PRESS, P.O. Box 1032, Oakville, Ontario, L6J 5E9, Canada. Offices and warehouse at 1252 Speers Road, Units #1&2, Oakville, Ontario, L6L 5N9, Canada and Mosaic Press, 85 River Rock Drive, Suite 202, Buffalo, N.Y., 14207, USA.

Mosaic Press acknowledges the assistance of the Canada Council, the Ontario Arts Council and the Dept. of Canadian Heritage, Government of Canada, for their support of our publishing programme.

The Canada Council | Le Conseil des Arts
for the arts | du Canada
since 1957 | depuis 1957

Copyright © Eugene McNamara, 1998
ISBN 0-88962-673-1
Printed and bound in Canada

MOSAIC PRESS, in Canada:
1252 Speers Road, Units #1&2,
Oakville, Ontario, L6L 5N9
Phone / Fax: (905) 825-2130

MOSAIC PRESS, in the USA:
85 River Rock Drive, Suite 202,
Buffalo, N.Y., 14207
Phone / Fax: 1-800-387-8992

E-mail: cp507@freenet.toronto.on.ca

MOSAIC PRESS in the UK and Europe:
DRAKE INTERNATIONAL SERVICES
Market House, Market Place,
Deddington, Oxford. OX15 OSF

WINTER APPLES

The tree has caught a kite
Which hangs like paper fruit
Beside those grave ornaments
The brown and puckered apples
Withered on the Bough.

from
For the Mean Time, (The Gryphon Press, 1965)

ACKNOWLEDGEMENTS

Some of these poems have appeared previously in the following magazines and anthologies:

Evidence, Prism international, Poem, Waves, Otherthan Review, Canadian Forum, RPM, Quarry, ARC, Unicorn, New, Niagara Magazine, Queens Quarterly, Poetry Toronto, Ontario Review, Poetry Canada Review, Cross Canada Writers Quarterly, University of Windsor Review, Writ, The Glass Cherry, Antigonish Review, Literary Review of Canada, The New Quarterly and Lobsticks (Alive Press, 1974) *Signatures* 1 (Nelson, 1976) *Flatsingles Press Broadside #2* (1976) *A Government Job at Last* (Macleod Books, 1976) *The Dominion of Love* (Polestar Press, 1998)

Some poems were collected in the following books:

For the Mean Time (The Gryphon Press, 1965)
The Dillinger Poems (Black Moss Press, 1971)
Hard Words (Fiddlehead Books, 1972)
Passages and Other Poems (Sono Nis Press, 1972)
Diving for the Body (Borealis Press, 1974)
Screens (Coach House Press, 1977)
Forcing the Field (Sesame Press, 1982)
Call it a Day (blewointmentpress, 1984)
The Moving Light (Wolsak & Wynn, 1986)

Grateful thanks is due to the editors and publishers of these publications.

For Margaret, with love.

"I dream our life, a thudding sound;
I take it outside in the rain: *everything.*
I hold my hands out: everything."

- William Stafford

CONTENTS

EUGENE MCNAMARA was born in Oak Park, Illinois in 1930. After attending De Paul University and Northwestern University where he received his Ph.D he emigrated to Canada and taught American literature and Creative Writing at the University of Windsor. McNamara founded the *University of Windsor Review* in 1965 and served as editor until 1987. Author of a dozen collections of poems and four collections of short stories, Eugene McNamara is Professor Emeritus in the Department of English at the University of Windsor and lives in Windsor with his wife Margaret.

the nineties
HOLDING A GOOD HAND

NEW POEMS

IN THE SPRINGHOUSE

Froth on milk in tall crocks
and the smell of butter the
smell of milk the smell of
shut in damp wood and my
feet bare on cool wet boards

The crocks stood in the shallow
spring and sunlight came in
through slatted cracks

Outside there were cattails
in the ditch and dragonflies
hung dazed in August heat
and my toes splayed on the
springhouse floor I thought
of the roads hot dust the
silence out there the far
off bank of clouds pressing
down pressing down beneath
tall heights of sheer sky

And here fifty years later
I think of all that is piled
up against what I think I am:
places I've been things I own
and remember that time driving
on Ventura Highway and the song
about it on the radio and I was
crowding the space working the
space singing *Hey! I'm still
here* driving toward the far
off bank of clouds my feet
remembering wet wood

ADAGIO

My voice turns like a key
rusty in an iron lock today
the radio is playing Albinoni
and I am staring out the
window at snow melting on
the garage roof where a cat
probes a tarred patch

Yesterday I rode the up
escalator watched the down
escalator fall endlessly
endlessly stairs pass like
song rising or falling and
today

On the screened-in front
porch winter light falls
on indoor-outdoor carpeting
light falls on white wicker
and Albinoni turns slowly

Out there steam rises from
the garage roof the cat has
lost interest in the patch
and is now intent across
the yard and metal stairs
are rising rising falling
falling like songs

IN THE GULLY

I am in the gully
close to the sparse
shards of spring snow
brown spikes of last
years weeds scraps
of old tough flaked
newspaper and

Across the stark field
my house hunches inside
its new grey siding and

Inside the house my wife
hums *I Fall to Pieces*

A print hangs in the
living room: three
intelligent eyed horses

A black and white rerun
is on tv a laugh track
of the dead rises—

Beside the house forsythia
urges itself and at school
my son is safe and learns
social studies the print
of the horses heads was
my grandmothers now

The light slants longer
across the field and my
windows are all on fire

My son is learning long
division

Soon the light will fail
and I will see the lights
of homecoming cars my son
coming home to learn that
geography is more than
distance and I will lie
down to wait for stars to
wheel and wink

In the orchard the trees
raise sleeping branches
free of last harvests
burden the grass is free
of crushed windfalls and
everything is waiting to
begin again
I am learning long
division

I am in the gully
close to every thing
I love.

ATGET'S GARDEN

I climb the crumbled steps
touch the lichened stone
and my eye hunches down
an avenue of bare trees.

Beyond the balustrade
is the hollow throat
of a dry fountain and
leaves on the steps are
flung like opened letters
on a table top nobodys
here I say to the rain
stained face of a statue.

At the end of the avenue
of trees Proust stands
at attention the way he
did after seeing Vermeer's
View of Delft: hat and
cane at his side—

slowly Proust bows to me
and I return the salute.

Between us the autumn
grass is like a hand held
out to test the weather—

I feel as if someone has
just or is about to
arrive and everything is
full of emptiness and
I stand like stone or
a man staring at the
shining roofs of a town
in a painting all gold
and green in summer light.

AT LOUIS SULLIVAN'S GRAVE

What had I come to say?
What did I expect to find?

Nearby tourists pose in
front of the Getty Tomb
and outside on Clark Street
a beer truck finds a spot
in front of the Kozy Tap
where architects on high
stools negotiate the
long afternoon and a girl
in a summer dress walks
between truck and tavern

The silence of the men
watching her follows
down the street like
someone sighing and far
to the west of here
where I put pennies on
the railroad track to
make them thin I was
a boy—now men lift
the glasses with shaking
hands I am not a boy

The tourists are gone
The girl is gone into
green summer light

Once I dreamed that girl
came to me in the rain
to say smiling *forgive*—
I had been stern as music
I took her in my arms

What did I expect to find?

Now I wish I had those
thin coins

LIVE ALL YOU CAN

Henry James sat high in the back of
Mrs. Whartons motor car eyes big and
ready to take in every morsel of Rye
and environs mufflered to the nose
ready to see every thing the way poor
Strether saw the French countryside
as if through a gilt frame like the
one he remembered in a dealers window
life seen as if through a frame of art

Take poor Strether falling in love
over an omelette aux tomates and
strawcolored Chablis love was this
complicated thing James might have
said to Mrs. Wharton as they putt—
putted along sex was difficult too
she might have answered she did not
inform him of her plans—

Back in London after dining with James
and after he left for his club the thing
happened: *the tryst*—

Edith Wharton was fortyseven when she
committed this first act of adultery
married for twentyfive years to poor
dull Teddy—

The act took place on the fourth of June
1909 in Suite Ninetytwo of the Charing Cross
Hotel a railway hotel with lots of quick
coming and going her lover was a cad who
went on to solace other women in other
hotels it was reputed that he solaced men
also he was not particular whom he solaced

Well James might have told her *comme
Il faut* do not be a *ficelle* in your
own life —life was not art sex like
love was complicated and sex like
art was not all it was reputed to be—

Take the sea he might have gestured
high in the motor car high above the
town and the coast all that coming in
and going out ceaseless not like poor
we whose coming and going has its firm
beginning and its promised end—

Charming Mrs. Wharton might have said
charming and she might have meant it—

IVES

Summer light on the river
moves and from far across
from steeples and mountains
come songs our fathers loved—

Mountains and rivers without end!

In the meadow by the river
girls will wash their hair
dry it in summer light and
toss it to the wind so it
will smell like a sailors
coat and the river flows
dark and brown and somber
as it falls to shallows
and the sea—

Mountains and rivers without end!

In the autumn evening there
is mist on the hills and songs
across the river are over the
hills and far away—

Mountains and rivers without end!

We stand in all weather
put out our hands to test
the air—there is early snow
on the gravestones and we
look up at the barn on the hill
and something takes us
by the throat—

the harvest—

Mountains and rivers without end!

DVORAK

There they are, the men in
heavy suits and slouch hats
the heavy men with beards
in 1909 dancing gravely—

At times the music is slow
sometimes quick but always
tender, restrained, like
a mothers hand on a childs
sleeping face—

The men are heavy like the
names of Bohemian food they
are like me walking with my
granddaughter who rushes at
everything—I move slowly—
I see the world full of sharp edges—

I want to be one of the men
the bearded men in Prague
in 1909 wearing heavy suits
and slouch hats who dance
to grave music—

FROM THE NEW WORLD

Dvorak came to America
four hundred years after
Columbus—

Dvorak saw Hoboken and
Cincinnati and Omaha
and Spillville, Iowa

Dvorak saw the Mississippi
and said *Crikey!* when he saw
Niagara Falls—

Freud and Jung boarded
the *George Washington* in
Bremen in 1909 and set
out for New York to bring
psychoanalysis to the
natives—Freud fainted
before the boat sailed—

Ravel listened to Jazz
in Harlem with Gershwin
and saw Edgar Allen Poes
house and Niagara Falls
and did not say anything
and saw the Grand Canyon
and did not faint—

SATIE

A woman dances by herself
in a dim afternoon room
slowly turning, slowly
bending hesitates—

A man on a train sees
her as the train slows
for the curve just past
her window seen swiftly—

His train had come into
the city past old yards
full of hollyhocks and
morning glory on fences—

Remembers walking at noon
in a foreign city all the
shops shuttered he walked
alone in high silent light—

Everything slouched together
at the end of the street
where he did not want to go
and a dandy came swaggering
around the corner wearing
a flower in his lapel—

FOR ROY ORBISON

1. The Specific Shapes of Loss

A boat was heading upriver trying to beat the ice
a gull was diving again again again swooping down
no luck swept up again on sunstruck white wings

The clouds closed again like an eyes wink and
the cars on the drive were incessant orderly
barely held in check all intent on their way
some place every one specific and alone—

None of this meant a damn thing after I heard—
something just left the world the way people
leave a room called away for some important
thing the way a movie screen goes dark—

I held the drab day in my hand held it tight
nobody said the word *lonely* like you did—
now I open my hand find it full of nothing.

I think of lonely men in bars staring at the
air in front of them listening to music they
didn't pay for don't especially want wonder
where they'll go next someplace they've never
been to now I hold the day as pure as your
words—

The diving gull breaks the water again again
my fogged up windshield is hit by sudden sun
light just as suddenly goes dark again and
in that moment all the windshields on the
drive were sunstruck open and I said *for ever*
green

2. Fifty-Two Pickup

A cruel grownups joke *hey kid*
want to play fifty-two pickup?
and then the four suits jacks on kings
a pack of lies thrown all over—

Those hard lessons of childhood—
being bullied shamed full of
fear all that hard stuff
to learn how to grow how
to love and live with loneliness—

fifty-two someone says *that's*
not so old—

Too soon I say looking
at everything spilled on
the floor waiting to
be picked up.

3. Level Crossing

The year has turned and I wait at the level
crossing cn cn norfolk & western cn cp erie
lackawanna illinois central for weeks now
I could not listen to your music it hurt cn
cn b & o chessie now I slide the tape in and
remember all the places filled with your song:

Kozaks tap the awcomon inn domas place the
6511 club pete ryans buddys lounge the q t
the ambush and the red lion the pass time
the billy goat the two eighty seven the
melody and mickeys midget cafe the keg room
the holiday house mother mckennas pinocchios
kys knotty pine inn duffys the horseshoe
the starlite room and the chatterbox—

Detroit toledo and ironton bangor and maine
santa fe cn cn great northern southern pacific
and the caboose the train is gone the tracks
are clear and I can go anyplace I want
I sit for a minute the cars behind me are
impatient I don't know where to go.

4. Holding a Good Hand

Another day: I stand in steel winter light
and stare at the empty river cant think of a
thing to say think I will remember this day
if I live through it as a big empty thing—

A boat passes me a high iron wall of rust
shutting off the skyline a big hand raised up
I raise my own hand to it say *here take this*
its all ive got—

The boat is past me now left me astern its
wake slaps the shore the river settles back
down and I think of the way a field fills up
with night and tree lines hunch down flocks
of birds rising from them and returning like
scattered words in a song you gave me *here*

Is a gift you said *take it* and I held your
word in my hand the way a field holds the dark
the way birds lift the trees and I open my
hand hold it up again your word rises from
my hand to the dying light.

FOR CHILDREN WHO DIED BY FIRE

(Our Lady of Angels School, Chicago, Illinois, 1958)

A father came to the ruin
three days after pounded
on the charred door called
Come out son! *Im here!*
but his son had passed his
voice the son who jumped
and fell to stone—

In one room twenty-four
dead children sat silent
at their desks hands on desk
tops clasped waiting to be
let go—

They are all gone past their
fathers voices now and the
Mass for the Holy Innocents
sung the coffins gone into
white winter sunlight—

The city held them awhile
then let them into darkness
the iron season turned and
Christmas trim and trees
were burned toys were lost
things broke down the decade
ended the world knelt down
waiting for new horror: men
who buried children in cellars
madmen on towers one dark
act followed another moving
into deeper dark—

I want to dream all children
back rising from the sidewalk
up into the burning air rising
to the windows and into the
rooms where fire hisses back
smoke draws into itself and
the childrens hands unfold
they are let go and down

they march backwards into
the yard back across the safe
street back safe to their homes
yawning breakfast back to bed
back to safe night sleep—

Now I call all fathers away
from the burned door say come
with me into this cold safe
night filled with sleeping
children—

The children do not fall but
are held up by their fathers
voices calling come out son
come home safe—

AS IMPERCEPTIBLY AS GRIEF

There is nothing to say
nobody to hear it still
my hands move rigid
I try for final words—

We kissed in the shadow of
the Moody Bible Institute
we were shameless—

Then her thin arms desperate
around me the tough traffic
went by on Torrance near
112th her arms close as
Stateline Road the August
sun was crazy as traffic
everything shook blazing
car radios on too loud—

Now I think of her lying
on a hill beside the river
and hunger as she did

Nothing will ever happen
again for the first time
I will walk near the night
river I want to call her
name I dont know her name

A friend said hey forget
it shes only a piece of ass
he said put her there and
shook my hand—

My Sunday sunburned girl
you were more
you were more
I know this now

I do not know your name
I did not put you there

BACK ON THE GROUND

I stood at the top of the high
steps looking out—the lake
was chilled blue the sky full
of sky the few clouds on the
horizon white as mainsails—

Time was as wide as the steps
and the girl down there at
the stone balustrade looking
out at the boats was pulled
by the wind her hair blazing
white as the flung water in
the fountain behind me and
a white and blue excursion
boat traversed the lake and
the girl turned to walk away—

It was like music or a word
in me that broke everything
hollowed in me and I wanted
to go down the steps I wanted
to stay where I was and so
I turned to see the fountain
water flung up like diamonds
in noon light I drank in the
air like cold water—

THE PISTOL CLUB

In the closedup Victory Tap
a mural of a beauty sitting
on a barrel of nails—

She sits on the rusty nails
and screws—

says the sign above
the mural—

The Ford Wyoming Drive-In
is closed too James Dean
cant say *hey now then there—*

Join our pistol club says
a sign in the Victory Tap
drink till twelve
piss till two—

I sang in the tall weeds
near the river *I picked you*
up in my pickup truck—

There was nobody particular
in mind nobody to hear me
sing and I cant sing
anyhow couldnt carry
a tune in a basket—

Hey I'll join the club
sit on the nails Im tough
as a pistol—

HEART LAND

—for Margaret

The geese in the park will not
migrate this winter—
They have forgotten how or why—

Its been months now since we
came home after thousands of
miles and two oil changes—

We kept stepping on the tracks of
Lewis and Clark and kept on crossing
the Missouri River over and over—

Have we changed at all?
There were those sheep in trucks
behind the Wranglers Cafe in
Wyoming mildly regarding us but
what could we do for them?

We had gone high on those
mountains and came down to sweet
water and a land full of sky—

Our squeegeed windshield let the
whole prairie into our laps and
a combine harvester in the Kansas
afternoon worried at the dry field—

Far from Alberta where we left our
son and far from Jackson where we
did not buy Million Dollar Cowboy
Bar tee shirts—two regrets—

Far from spiked purple flowers
in the ditches of North Dakota
where sloughs crowded the roads
edge and the sky was wide awake—

If tomorrow comes and I wake to
find you next to me I'll know I am
home—

If tomorrow never comes again well
weve been there and back again—

You are the country I will never ever
fly from like geese in the park close
to home you are the map of far places
home in my heart—

MATINS

Bells in faroff steeples
summon and birds announce
morning—

bellsong birdsong—

Come and walk with me my
love listen to what my eyes
sing to you: I will not
let you go—

As a man carries a glass
of water to his child in
the night—not a drop will
fall the bough will not
break we shall gather at
the river—

Remember the dry light
over the ocean and the
long grass in morning
light and wild ponies
running on the beach
plunging in the surf
their manes shaking
in the wind?

Remember the prairie
swift seen between
the freight cars?

The prairie will be there
when the trains long gone
the ponies will be there
when we return—

Here are trees shaking
swaying in the wind and
staying in calm silence—

Train horns in the hills
the hoarse muttering of
the river where it falls—

What I hold in my hands—
not a drop will spill and
the bough will not break
and we shall gather at
the river and I will not
let you go—

LOCAL MAN WEDS CHICAGO MAIDEN
(from the *Berwyn Life,* 1952)

That wild enraged swan
that chased my wife up
a hill when she was a
child didnt get her but
I did—

That year in Berwyn Park
I sat with my father
watching semipro ball had
peanuts no salt stale as
the summer air—

The train went past up
on the embankment hurtling
silver going who the hell
knew where we were all
still back there in the
bleachers—

The swan went where swans
go my wife grew up her
big eyes bigger than when
she ran up a hill into
my arms oh my dear I said
my heart frantic as wings—

YOU'LL NEVER KNOW

When my wife is away
I still sleep on my side—

If I wake in the night
her side is a big vacant
silent space like a place
where a tooth was pulled—

Gently I place my tongue
in the empty place so
it wont hurt—

DESTINATIONS

From my place under the bridge I could
look up and think about the stories
of people flinging themselves off
hanging themselves oh all this long
ago back when people went crazy in
the winter blew their heads off with
gunpowder fed arsenic to the family
ran off with salesmen went to Chicago
turned trollop my aunts spoke of all
this in whispers hoping to shield me—

Dennis and I made our First Communions
I tried not to have sinful thoughts
hoped I would not forget in the middle
of the night take a drink of water
and a fine rain was falling I had a
terrible urge to stick out my tongue—
Marie Alice demure eyes downcast in
front of me I thought of her mothers
iron cooling on the board at home and
all over town irons standing on boards
cooling—

Illinois you were a thorn in my heart

Out near the towns edge I pumped gas
at the Texico read Thomas Wolfe all
night yawned all day some nights could
not stand it said *o lost*! and swam in
the night river so different from the
the simple placid creek in daylight we
skipped stones across sat under the
bridge listened to cars rumbling over
on the way to Joliet or further but
at night the river had no bottom my
skin shrinks and crawls as I remember
Dennis wondered if taking stuff from
the dime store was a mortal sin we
wanted war dreamed of war in that
summer and Dennis drowned in that
river

I loved the movies with wet sidewalks
after rain neon lit high heel, click
echoed skirt flicked above the puddles—
in a room above the street I lay on
the bed curtains hung tired out neon
flicks I lie smoking of course staring
at the ceiling of course not looking
at the woman in the black slip curled
asleep at my side my eyes are on
something distant about to be shown
in flashback.

So I grew up watching those exciting
fast girls in my class—Tillie Dolly
Lolly—all those names ending in
teeth clenched groin clenched *eee*
like cousin Susie all beautiful and
out of reach Susie posed under a tree
flowering in Uncle Buds back yard.

I learned useful things from Uncle Bud
watched him frown at the thermometer
snap a skeptical finger at it *ninety
two? not hardly*—

Uncle Bud beat his wife everybody
said so he told me to be a man I
remembered it when doors clumped
shut outside the church the day of
his funeral it was ninety-five in
the shade.

Once listening to truck loads of
hogs cross the river heading north
to the yards I alone remembering
Dennis and a bus went across kids
yelling out the window down at me
and a girls face smiling down they
had been maybe to Lincolns tomb and
she was bored out of her mind rolling
her eyes at Vera dying for a smoke
the guide told them for godssake what
kind of marble and how goddam much
and who was that boy down there—

The girl on the bus would be named
Dolly or Susie or Tillie—

I remember a winter when the pipes
froze and the small plane crashed
and sadness spread like a stain
from Clear Lake Iowa

That winter I met a girl whose name
was not Susie or Dolly—

Out near the Des Plaines River we
parked it was in public private
and dangerous all around us the red
eyes of taillights staring we groped
and fumbled to radio light the music
full of our deep shallow breathing.

We rose from the seat ready to come
back into the public world and the
forms of children not yet born whined
in back of us for asking for fast food
asking for promises to make chances
to take charging the high price of
loving.

Just the other day I thought the
ship is given to darkness and the
sea and I remembered Dennis and my
Uncle Bud and Shorty is dead and

Stash lives in Florida and Knudsen
is in the Golden Valley Nursing
Home and Dolly and Susie are god
knows where and my children are
grown and gone and I wonder if
the river still runs under the
bridge

LEAVING THE RUST BELT

A tall brick tower on
the closed creamery beside
the river a clock face
on all four sides each
telling the same time
saying *time* is *money*
its noon break or quitting
time

Past the falls the river
settles down takes a breath
after all the hurlyburly
tumult becomes placid
serene as an old man
taking his morning walk

The river bends past
the towns end like an
elbow on the window
sill gentle friendly

Once the falls turned
wheels and belts slapped
on spools day and night
three shifts split time
by whistles but today
no shifts no time clocks
punched nothing but
belts hanging from the
spools in cracked light
no wheels turn the
falls drop for nothing

In Ft. Mitchell Kentucky
the Holidome pool was empty
the whirlpool on the fritz
there was an ice storm
the ice machine hummed all night

In downtown Nashville the
bellman warned us not to
walk at night but we did
and found a fern piano bar
all the country musics
out of town the bartender
said
After Andrew Jacksons home
Graceland was simple

The whirlpool at the Tanque
Verde Inn in Tucson worked
just fine

In the frothing water I
thought about the man I
saw on Ezzard Charles Blvd
standing in front of the
boarded up place staring
at the sign *checks cashed*
anytime

We did not stop at the
Casey Jones Village

Call this a sanrich says
the man who ordered the
Senior Special *If I held*
this pork chop to the light
you could see through it

I agree with him

Why not? We'll never see
each other again not
in this world

This road is sure tough
its mean as a motel towel

Things I learned:

Times are tough all over

Andrew Jackson Elvis
and Casey Jones are dead

Elvis had a twin brother
died at birth

Never order the Senior Special

All the countrys music
is out of town

WEST OF TUCSON

Kentucky and Tennessee are far
behind us and the Buford Pusser
Museum closed Mondays and the
Theater of Great River Disasters
closed Mondays

Now for ten miles we are promised
BEST BOOTS BEST PRICES and a free
rattlesnake ranch

At the TURN HERE sign we exit
onto an Old West town street
where late afternoon sun bakes
the still air and we go into
an almost cool dim interior

On the postcard rack Pancho Villa
rides in sepia and impassive stone
eyed Indian chiefs stare at a girl
holding up a *My Parents Went to
Arizona* tee shirt the girl
says *Gee I dont know—*

Outside a man asks me if that is
Casa Grande over there and I say
I dont know Im not from around
here and he says nobody is

My picture is taken in front of
a fake saloon the girl has bought
the tee shirt her friend says *those*
boys were really excellent—
we have not bought any boots

The sun slants lower and across
the highway tall saguaro stand
like tired old grandees

A month later the film is developed
and there I am squinting at what
I do not remember and the evening
was coiling like a dormant snake
It is all blurred now like a postcard
rack slowly spun and still saguaro
stand in stiff dignity keeping watch
for us in the dark

COMING INTO VAN NUYS

I look ahead and see it as
a bowl of orange light and
I am part of a rosary of
tail lights going down down
the radio says *we'll never
forget you till somebody new
comes along*—

Orange—
I think of oranges held in
an old woman's hands at the
corner of Venice Boulevard
the light changed I had no
time to buy them I've tasted
them all the way since—

And there is my exit!
I am coming into Van Nuys!

The city is a bowl of orange
light and I am in the exit
lane and I think of oranges
they must have been heavy
in her hands all day on the
island so heavy in her hands—

I am in my driveway engine
off I still hold the wheel tight
I wish I could have
lifted the oranges from her
hands

HIBISCUS

Bloomed in the courtyard
of the Oakwood Apartments—

There was the unending moan
of traffic on the freeway—

Someone walked through
the courtyard heels echoed
on the walk then silence
again a distant door closed—

On tv across the pool faint
delighted laughter rose and
bloomed—

The hibiscus didnt listen
drooping open as kissed
lips in the fragrant dark—

MAGIC TAP, MANTENO, ILLINOIS

The bartenders eyes are shuttered down
his face could smile if he wanted to

He is the tall linchpin that holds
this place together

We lean forward on our stools
We are like the rows of rubbed glasses
The firm line of bottles that wait

It's just past noon and hitting ninety
Outside the sidewalks shimmer and buckle

Lemons are sliced olives laid out
Businessmen are leaving the offices
wondering what the special of the day
is at the Magic Tap

They will call the bartender by name
He will incline his head and almost
smile

His face says silently
take courage

At the state facility the lawns are
sun scorched and no light comes in
the barred windows and a game show
is on tv the same show is on at
the Magic Tap nobody watches

Afternoon comes to town like an
old gunfighter trying to quit
and here in the Magic Tap we lean
on the bar keeping time not hoping
for any magic

PEORIA, 1927

In downtown Peoria you could
fry an egg on the sidewalk at noon

It hasnt rained for a month
and morning smells as soggy
as room 302 in the Olinger Hotel
where a textbook salesman groans
and turns over to find last
nights whore has left already.

She carries her shoes out
to the hallway puts them on

The elevator operator yawns
pretends not to be interested
as she steadies herself against
the wall to raise a foot to a shoe
he gets a whiff of knee as she
smooths her skirt down he opens
the gate *down?* he smiles
she doesnt smile back why
should she he aint the paying
kind of fellow.

A month ago it rained so much
the river overflowed and a boy
fell down a sewer was shot into
the river he did not survive.

Now the sewers are hollow dry
aching for rain

Miss Hewitt raises both arms
to push the hair off her neck
sighing thinks of Mozart and
that salesman who must be married
of course and all the boys
in the eighth grade classroom lean
forward to watch Miss Hewitt
and the slow pulse in her neck.

A fat blue fly bumps at the
window screen the empty corn
stalks in the fields hang limp
the salesman dreams of water
tunneling under him
a woman comes out of
the Olinger Hotel walking
slowly in the hot morning.

Everyone agrees: its going
to be another scorcher.

SO LONG

The late August sky
clear as a childs eye
and the light at the
top of the tree is a
shaking green fire—

Shadows on the lawn are
fingers slowly spread
and the girl next door
is learning to ride her
bike in the driveway and

My neighbors tomatoes
ripen or not when they
feel like it his blue
wheelbarrow lies on its
side all tuckered out—

Now the tree that was
bent down by last springs
snow is touched by final
light it hasnt rained in
weeks my umbrella hangs
in the closet and I say

So long to all this and
the sky holds last light
lingers and the season
yawns and turns over—

AUTUMN

Octobers end and leaves
clustered are rained on
turned to meal—

The creeping sense of on
coming snow and I wake at
night to a moments dread
and the soughing trees—

Oh in the morning I can
lean towards the day and
swagger at noon—

This hunched human heart
yearns and yearns still
this hungered hankering
towards what?

The turning away from the
arched sky the big fields
and wide waste space there
between hopeful houses—

Tall grass on the edge of
small rivers that always
and forever run to larger
waters—

There is where I want to go

with the river—

NOVEMBER SNOW

Last night I marked each leafs
calm descent and walked towards
the river which went where rivers
go and then the snow began—

Today the simple sun gives me a hand
and there are no tracks in the yard
and still the river goes where rivers
go and empty ships sit there waiting
high and still waiting for something
to happen and I wait with them—

CONTINENTAL DIVIDE

We drove all night in an ache
of dark space and lights far
ahead—-Cutbank—

Then Cutbank is behind us
small point of light going
out and a freight train
past us the other way
a sudden rush of light
and bulk and big dark—

And finally there is Shelby
and we sink into our room
there is a power failure
I get the flashlight from
the car its been bad news—

The parking lot is full of
pickup trucks and I stand
in the lot full of trucks
and stars and say *I am here*
say *I am home*-—

THINGS TO SEE

A watertower with a name on it
seen across the fields is not
expected—

There is a museum there of
everyday farm life a hundred
years ago the tower is an
interruption not expected not
quite a surprise in a tedium
of similar things seen—

I could stop there turn off
and stop stand at the curb
breathe in icy air walk to
the museum find it closed find
the diner full of men in
hunting caps—

Or none of this go on the
tower behind me smaller in
my rearview forget the name
of the town leave all this
a hundred years behind—

HOW BEAUTIFUL UPON THE MOUNTAINS

Traveling north of the storm
the seared sky over the pass
a final fall of light—

The sky and the mountain range
are seamless and the roadside
culvert is full of old snow—

The air is full of wings and
I say *earth* and *forever*—

I descend to the valley floor
the mountain tops still hold
the sun and all below is a
bowl of light I shift into
low and go down to the light

PLAINSONG

They are cooking mash
at the distillery today
and white gulls drop
down to the water next
to the tall silos—

We drive through steam
clouds come out at the
bend in the river and
tall buildings over
there hold afternoon
light—

And the white silos the
rivers casual bend birds
circling sailing down
ships passing there—

Behind the bridge is sky
Behind the sky is a word—

CLARITAS

Mother was tired so
she lay down and
did not get up again—

It was a hard thing—

Here she said *here*
I am—

I went to the swollen
river and tried to say
here—
The solemn summer
noon silent as heaven—

It was a place where
things went to die—

Rank creek water
iron and cold the
rot of leaves and
vines—

When I was a child
I came down here to lie
down in shallows—

Saw light come down
through hanging leaves—
it gave me the
gift of distance—

Now there is a cold
bird in the hedge—
birds hunched on the
power line—

I say *here*—

KEEPING IN TOUCH

Sometimes I hear my mothers
voice again—

I have not been called in twenty
years—she lies back there in
the earth of home—

But all those times I think:
wrong number bad connection—
I hear my mother singing in a
chorus of young voices coming
through the dark wire intent
insistent—

Telling me to walk down the
straight path to the creek
pointing to the furrows in
the field running out to where
the land touches sky—

This is a certain field she
says and this is for your
own good—

Goodbye I say and hang up
leave my hand on the phone
waiting for the call keep
in touch she says keep in
touch—

SNOW DOWN HOME

They tell strangers not to
try to get to the mailbox
in a storm many have tried
gone and died on the way—

That snow is confusing
like God gone nuts—

Come summer and corn
tassels hang in sunshock
you remember the snow
and almost miss it—

Take the hired man who
showed up at harvest
time worked my uncles
field ate dinner with
the family didnt say where
he had been nobody asked—

After the harvest he up
and left next fall he
didnt come back nobody
asked where he was where
he had gone—

Like someone who went out
in the blizzard trying
to find the barn or go
back home just went out—

THERE IS A FOUNTAIN FILLED WITH BLOOD

It began with melting snow
clumped on branches dropping
to fall pooling and

Seeking between and through
to fall swelling and this
aching hurl through a flume
all froth spume—

Now slow and clear and
I can count the rocks and
I put my hand into the water
cold as a bite into an apple
and I raise my shocked hand
to the tall sky and know
that I belong here—

I say there it is
and there it goes—

My mother sang a hymn in
the backyard as she hung sheets—

The sheets bellied like sails
on ships going away—

LONG TIME GONE

The last light falls on mossy
gravestones the names already
blurred with snow—

Ive been a long time gone—

Im back here now and snow
falls on a horses back he
moves away from the fence
between breaths and still
snow moves with him across
the field—

Everything has come back here
among the stones where things
end and begin to hurt—

It was a day of long shadows
and a long drive past fields
full of frost on the corn
shocks—a long time—

No use to call the horse
I dont know his name or
remember the names of those
already gone—

I stand still in the silence
thinking:

I would not have missed it
for the world but who will
see it after me?

Ive been a long time gone—

the seventies
MOVING DAY

POEMS FROM:

Outerings (Delta Canada, 1970)

The Dillinger Poems (Black Moss Press, 1971)

Passages and Other Poems (Sono Nis Press, 1972)

Diving For the Body (Borealis Press, 1974)

Screens (Coach House Press, 1977)

DARK AT THE CLOSING

Like a traveler sailing the Archipelago who sees the
luminous mists lift
toward evening, and little by little makes out the shore, I
begin now to
discern the profile of my own death.—

The Emperor Hadrian

Portents:

a dead crow on the wet porch steps—

a dead starling by the curb's edge
day by day growing flatter, drier,
more an abstract of a bird's shape—

a dead squirrel in the bushes
one eye socket already filled
with ants, blind, impervious
now and beyond reach—

a dead young rabbit caught
in the mower's fury

I study the pulse in my wrist
read the obituaries and
subtract my age from theirs.

My talk is all of rare disease
and sudden death:
His age? I ask. *Only forty?*
Only sixty? Twenty? Only—

I subtract my father's age
at death from mine
and wonder:

I am as cold as early morning feet
on bare linoleum.

The Situations:

A man falls asleep while his children watch television.
The voices, speaking of super heroes, evil princesses
and the planet Thoth, enter his dreams.

The rain-scattered birds
return to the tree.

The things I gave:
A word. a touch.
What were they?
They break in your hands.
Let them free.

Others raise their faces to
the sky as bells peal and
silver jets pierce the tall sky.

The faces are filled with
intent joy or wonder or
fear of what the bells or
the planes outward bound
mean, what they say,
what is to come.

The faces lift the sky.

I begin now to taste
my own death.

("We can't return.
We can only look behind
from where we came—")

all that summer it rained
I thought I'd lost you.
Been trying to reach you.
You couldn't hear.
I was shouting down
a dry well.

Bubbles rise in the blood
fine as silk urged along
the corridors under the skin
pulsed through the body's
labyrinth towards the heart
unwinding dreaming threads
of unloosening, falling
away, apart, coming towards
the end of themselves and
of my time.

My thoughts hesitate at this:

The dark mystery of a train shed
where steam idly boils across
grease-wet concrete.
The dark cars are silent
and unmoving.

full circle? the blood
does not answer but sullen
pulses on in its own dark
bemused in its own journey
through me towards silence
in my heart.

the cars in the train shed!
they too are portents!
they are mysterious and unmoving!

At the Closing:

a few measures:

a father carries his sleeping son
out of the car after a long trip
home. the child awakens for a
moment, is confused by starlight
and turns deeper into sleep.

a child traces a word in a book
ball: does he think of roundness?
of the shape of his hand curved to
hold?   of the earth?
of the earth unheld by any hand
but let drop spinning alone?

time enough for that later.
for now it is enough
that he trace the word
that his lips celebrate the thing
that he turn from the word
that he go running into
the world and time.

LEARNING TO PLAY
THE ACCORDION

you wanted a guitar but somehow ended up with that
ridiculous box of air   you didnt practice enough
each lesson was a fumble of agony your teacher
exasperated and silent reached a thick hand over
your shoulder pointing at notes you hunched to peer
at guessed wrong he sighed like the last drawnout note
as the box closed

at the first recital you began ok but then you became
aware: the sound coming from you wasnt the same as
from the others and you tried to catch up or slow down
it was all blurring and the others seemed to be leaning
as far away from you as they could will it never finish

it did of course and you were in the back seat on the
way home and your father cleared his throat and your
mother

said *what happened?* you said you didnt know you looked
down at your helpless hands lying there no use to men-
tion
the guitar

later when your mother died you wanted to say *what
happened*
no answer   just the squeezed air in the room coming in
going out in a sigh of wrong notes

MY FATHER CALLS ON
MY MOTHER ON AN
AFTERNOON IN 1926

this is the day
he proposed and it
has become a late
tv show on an old
seventeen inch set
with the horizontal
hold slipping sudden
storms of snow burp
gun bursts of static
i am not dreamed of
yet my father wears
a new suit with a
vest and a high collar
he looks like buster
keatons sidekick if
i didnt know the end
i would think its
a comedy with the
camera jumping around
and they move too
fast down the walk
down the street
sudden closeup the
smiles shy and
lingering and people
whipping past the

camera and shots of
traffic quick as fish
in the silent din of
all those chugging motors
there is a moustache
policeman john l
sullivans face the
essex the packard
saloon cars rumble
seats spare tires
on the side everybody
smiles for the camera
my mother and father
are at an amusement pier
designed by burnham &
root with all kinds of
green wrought iron
they are feeding something
to a monkey half bending
my mother is holding
the monkey it is a parody
of me waiting for my
turn and i cry out
but the organ grinder
smiles and keeps on
cranking there they are
by a railing where a life
preserver is hung with
the name of the pier on it
the sun glares on the water
it is setting darkness
and strings of light bulbs

my father shooting a rifle
mother holds the prize kewpie
doll which again reminds me
monkey doll child
could this film be run
backwards the monkey jumping
out of her arms the cars
in swift reverse they jog
backwards up the walk
to my mothers door
my fathers hat lifted
the door closes his
finger pulls back from
the bell he backpedals
up the street and saves
himself from the future
even as i ask the film
stops and begins again
relentless they are made
to walk down the street
in the dead summer sunshine
made to feed the monkey
stand by the life preserver
shoot the rifle win the
prize again i cannot
even turn the set off when
the film ends and they
play the signing off anthem

DILLINGER LEAPING

the figure in
the straw boater
his suit jacket
buttoned all the way
his face floating in
the tall dry air
above his collar
not needing to brace
himself on the bank
counter vaulting slowly
not needing to hold the
rim of the straw hat
the gun held loosely
his face floating in
a mask of unconcern
brute matter overcome
by his high sailing
high easy jumping
floating face set
and serious and the
hat is pure circus
what muscles bunched
extended mutually
precise and pure he
leaps and history
falls apart lies
at his feet as he
jumps high there
a figure in the air
higher than death

DILLINGER'S CAMERA

at the world's fair:
taking snapshots
of camels and policemen
posing with his girl
smiling in the lakeside sun

the black box sheltered
with a half-curved palm
against his vest
his head bent peering
the finger hesitates hovers

got it

everything breathes again
the spool is wound the
black in red number
reveals itself ready
to go on
poised
receptive
to record whatever he
wished to make final
camels policemen girlfriends

got it

caught fixed instant final
stopped
as he never was
I see him moving
with the speed of brightness

just there   there
beyond the edge
like an absent cousin
from the party photo

running to get away
from the final pose
until all the cameras
of the world clicked

                            got him

still at last
held by cigars
in vests and straw hats
his dyed hair sneering
his moustache smiling

the camera leaps from
his opened fingers
dancing into the sun

aims down on a world
no longer fair
wild
running

he is beyond
all cameras now
waiting like a man
in a drug store
for his prints

waiting now
who at last
posed so easily

never dreaming why

DIVING FOR THE BODY

I

there was my mothers
fathers farm near a canal

(divers went in after
a car drunk night driven
into the green deep)

1938 down there walking
through cattail insect
noise saw a snake make an
s on the water

1940 new phone line in
side plumbing no more
walk to squeak rust pump
no more outhouse jokes

1960 sold
now home for disturbed
antisocial children or
nuclear power plant
something i forget
exactly

not mine anymore
it never was

(found the car
never found
the body)

II

"i am sleepy and the oozy weeds about me twist"

the canal soothes gentle
moves on secret towards
the rivers towards the
larger waters giving up
its patient dead its mined
earth its secrets

the children who live in the sea
their hair rising among tendrils
of seaweed curving curled
in the currents spend their days
turning in the deep among curious
fish sleeping on the current
dreaming of other lives on shore

ocean is full of bodies
some sit in their sunken
boats crusted with coral
playing final game of statue
in the green twilight
others are lately come
they are the restless ones
bumping and rising in the
slow light they tumble
over the sandy floor
resting awhile on the
mossy rocks not caring
that the fish now prod
at them darting to their
eyes and then their hands
waving impatient at first
then final accepting

III

i wait for resurrection
for the sea to give up its
dead children plunged seaward
there is no promised rising
the secret sea holds us fast
in watery arms the children
sing in their long sleep
coral crusts thicker on the
seated men rocking in their
patient boats time slows
down the blood slows seeping

so we named the waters
traced them on maps saying
here it began and there it
falls and enters as if we
could hold them safe and sure
probing at the rivers mouth
i find the lost channel
choked with algae bedsprings
a junked truck on its side
door gaping in amazement
pushing through! passage
must be found through the
choking weeds the persistent
all down pulling green feeling
mesh reluctant final letting
go and up the canal back to
where it started the shoal
water all clotted dank debris
silted over the clean bones
of indians and animals who
were dredged up put down again
to rest and now grinning at
me as i pass but i do not stop
i pass day and night i will
rise in a tall shower of waking
water now surface broken taken
high in the new air the water
falling back falling silver
shivering to lie quietly again
and rising i see earths scar
healed and i cry out there is

THE FACTORY

the factory was where the men
in the cool mornings went
coming out of doors
wives and children already
turned to their own lives
screen doors closing

your father
the man next door
across the street
all the men were
leaving for the factory
saying *morning*
as they unlocked
their car doors
bent to go in
to the factory

they drove without sunglasses
they carried a lunch
they said *morning*
but leaned towards
afternoon
and gathered darkness

you wondered about it
you waited for your turn
to be one of them
one of the men
leaving a house
in the cool morning
to go to the factory
saying *morning*

have you found the factory
now have you penetrated
its mysterious gates are
its engines shuddering into
life   its air blue with
burned metal your hands
sparking your head bent
to work your lips moving
silently in the engines
roar silent saying
morning morning morning

IN THE NOON CHILL

waiting in the chill noon
for the switch to drop the
coal car watching the breath
cloud in the still air
then the steel rumble of
the car groaning on the grade
the engine eases it jolts
once locked brake uncoupled
and then seeing the under
side of the wheel rubbed
silver the flange rubbed the
tracks top edge rubbed silver
the bolted plates the numbers
net and tare date of construction
the congruence of all he feels
the weight of the car on the
wheel at the point where the
wheel meets the track a point
of great pressure nothing can
unhook it ease it and he feels
afraid in the chill noon sun

SUMMER IN THE
CECO STEEL CORPORATION

leaving the plant in
the summer afternoon
the sun already old
feeling the knees quiver
bewildered in light
the blued panes of
factory glass give
light back someone is
sweeping up around
the machines curls of
metal in the oil i am
going past store fronts
there is a bar with
photos of the war curling
on the mirror i am waiting
for my bus too tired to
notice the girl in shorts
eating a green popsicle
it is melting faster than
she can suck already i am
thinking about tomorrow
morning ice drips on her
chin i think of morning
and engines starting ice
falls on the hot concrete

SPRING CLEANING

to a peaceful opening of
winter windows i admire
the order of things:
diesels coming down the
bridge my windexed glass
startling the halfnaked
yard those birthday flowers
i gave you dead a week later
lying in the morning coffee
grounds they had the same
going away look you had

i remember on just such
a day holding my breath
cycling past the tb hospital
going out to find a place
in the woods where i could
lie down and think about
meeting you and the order
of things

soon it will be summer and
ill be moving a lawn sprinkler
out there the water falling
like flung diamonds in the sun
the diamonds id like to dress
you in now i think i cant
imagine a world without you
in it a world like a day
without music no flowers
in the ground

MOVING DAY

there is one last load in
the centre of the living room
curtain rods a shower curtain
a box of photos proving that
someone lived here an empty
fishbowl a broom

the living room: dead and
final now i am the only
sound left as i go through
shocked open rooms walls
stripped and shy

outside is as casual as ever
my muscles keep the ache of
each thing possessed and taken
out i bend to put the box in
the car some curled pictures
fall out on the autumn grass
there we are on another moving
day hopefully smiling into the
future not knowing how cleaning
house how brooms sweep down
so long a way how we might miss the
places weve been the places we
are going towards

TATTOO

there is a tattooed rose on my left arm it grows in the dark
blooms in the winter the knife on my right arm waits to cut it
wants to cut something the rose is silent in its skin the knife
is helpless i lie on the knife then on the rose then on my plain
back i feel the needles move on my chest making thorns a branch
growing in blood towards the promised meeting

IN THE BALLOON FACTORY

Rushing to daylight. Late for work. I am bicycling
desperately. Ahead of me I see myself. No shirt on
zipping along no hands not wondering if the balloon
factory is hiring again.

Then at noon. Lunch in the balloon factory. Stella
rolls an orange on the table. Slowly. Makes it easier
to peel. The orange like a tart balloon opens and the
air is full of its taste.

Afternooon. Killing time. Slumping towards.

Overtime. The machine slides in an ecstacy of oil.
The rubber stretches in orbs, drooping flaccid in
resigned heaps at the end of the line, sorted into boxes
labeled **blue** and **red** and the machines rise in higher
ecstacy and finally fall falling fall into sudden silence.
The balloons wait for celebration.

LATE NIGHT

You let in the night air
and far off a car starts
coughing thoughtfully

All over town words are
falling down and now
you are riding the
horses of sleep

The car is going past
tired and resolute
it is gentle in the

dark going

the eighties
SAYING GRACE

POEMS FROM:

Forcing the Field (Sesame Press, 1982)

Call it a Day (blewointmentpress, 1984)

The Moving Light (Wolsak and Wynn, 1986)

PUNCHING IN

1

kuperitis is sick the dispatcher says
so your helper takes his route today —
jesus the driver says lays his order
book on the counter you mean i got
this new man today? jesus he looks
at me shakes his head sighs well lets
go jesus god why me damm a new man
then out in the truck he laughs says
listen dont worry this route is pussy
we bounce away from the dock my arm
on the hot window ledge listen he says
we'll go through this route like shit
through a tin horn and now im for some
reason happy

PUNCHING IN

2

shorty knows all the right moves always
carry a wrench he says always be going
someplace or coming back now he leans
his chair back against the panel closes
his eyes he has stuff propped all round
the door so larsen has to bump into it
and we'll hear him coming then shorty
jumps up grabs the clipboard reads the
dials and i check the water gauges we're
busy as hell looking serious then larsen
leaves shorty sighs back into his chair
tells me stories about oriental women

PUNCHING IN

3

the coal car was being shunted down and
i watched my breath in the sharp air
and the look of the engineer who raised
one gloved hand in salute and the brakeman
swung off and threw the switch and backed
off and the diesel humped the car towards
the spot but the car was beginning to rock
and it was teetering on one side and then
the other and then was over slowly and
the diesel stood shuddering and a black
wave of coal washed across the yard
burying the tracks and the switch and
the brakeman danced out of the way and
the air was full of dust and the ground
shocked and then there was no noise but
the throb of the diesel and my breathing

PUNCHING IN

4

the coal silo moves the clouds
and i have to climb the silo the
grease gun against each rung as
i climb my eyes on the deltas of
rust running from each bolt in
the concrete and i go up and then
on the top the whole sky opens
and soars now the grease gun to
the conveyor's nubs and a snake
of new grease hangs from the gun
drops to the silo's roof and on
the noon height sudden the air
is full of whistles answered by
church bells and from the national
baking company the smell of bread
and i stand and turn in the singing
air filled with hunger and joy
joyful hunger ringing singing

PUNCHING IN

5

the first day on the welding line
and there go two of the tough motor
cyclists from twentysecond street
they've just been hired not for this
line please godalmighty   they beat
the shit out of people just for fun
and then at lunch they all sit on
the same skid and the motorcyclists
smile say hows it going

PUNCHING IN

6

knudsen never smiles his eyes are
always angry he says his philosophy
of life is never to take shit even
from the boss or your wife listen
are you married kid   well get all
the nooky you can while you're able
its all long hours and short pay
slow horses and fast women kid

IN THE RAILROAD YARD

in the railroad yard the old
red cars wear their names
vaguely   cp   lackawanna &
delaware illinois central they
lie in a sleep so deep nobody
can wake them the old men with
bent brass cans gently touch
their bearings with new oil
those old men whose faces wear
no names but somehow say
all those places too

AT THE END OF THE DAY

at the end of the day
i stand in the stricken
air ready to run for it
the birds fly from one
tree to another it doesnt
make sense to me but i
suppose they know what
they are doing someone
has pulled out my plug
and the engines have
shut down im empty like
a machine shop at night
under the eyes of mice
i want to sigh like the
last gush of steam in
the engine the astonished
boiler hollow with itself
i dont know where im supposed
to be now or where you are
reluctant i have to move
i regret all i did not do
today the day is floating
away a ferry leaving the
slip im on the dock the wake
settles back in quiet folds
you are on the far shore
im here at the end of the day.

NINETEEN FORTY-SIX

Sunday summer ballgame
radioed out the porch
window to me lying in
the sun volume set too
low for the score only
a drone of one mans dry
voice against a crowds
low roaring and im too
lazy to get up and turn
it higher i dont give
a damn anyhow all week
a wheelbarrow precarious
balanced pulling me to
the dumping space now
my muscles pull me down
into the grass and the
roaring rises a hit!
a hit fair ball going
over a high wall but
i dont care shrugging
deeper in the sun into
the grass pouring my
self into it dont give
a damn and now i soar
like a fair ball high
over all walls

SHIFT END

Walking down cicero avenue
i do not look at the sign
in the kozy tap *continuous*
entertainment i carry my
coat wrapped this morning
around my tired shoulders
now i am not thinking of
a single thing the after
noon shift is already half
an hour older so
am i

Willy and vince have gone
to the beach i think of
them getting sunburned
meeting girls not thinking
about me walking cinders
crunching under my shoes
white hot sidewalk up
there is 12th street and
the streetcar i wanted
to catch leaving

I pass a building named
muriel 1931 there is a
clock in the basement
window inside the clock
two plastic children
on swings tick and tock

Somedays nobody winds
the clock and the swings
dont move the children
hang still waiting

Last summer one night
we drove to wisconsin
for ice cream hoping
for girls and beer on
the way nothing but
fat bugs slapping to
death lights along the
white line lying placid
there not promising a
damn thing

Now 12th street is near
lights change in a roar
of gears in late light
nobody winds my clock my
feet fly over this white
walk i am thinking of far
off Wisconsin where girls
swim in ice cream and beer

Here there is only a shift
ending gears shifting and
a man going home
nothing changes
i hang on the afternoon
like a child on a swing

SQUARE DANCING IN NAPERVILLE

for Dan Dungan

Forming the square you wondered
about the quakers — about sex —
and you honoured her and dipped

If it feels good do it said the
song but you weren't sure as you
allemained whirling saw the
crash doors in the high school
gym gleam with new varnish her
thighs under a sashay of bright
cotton and you led to the right
circled in a line and came on
back home and do-si-doed

Later in the hallway you looked
in at the dark machine shop
found the door open went in to
kiss among silent drill presses
circular saws hung on the walls
in moonlight *did you ever lie
and listen to the rainbow* echoed
from the gym your armpits damp
mouths open you honoured her

Well dan we've promenaded down
years pretty good since that
night you swung her in the circled
squares and bowed to her in the
hallway under the framed portraits
of longfellow bryant and whittier

A boy in danville broke my heart
she said and later going home on
the chicago aurora & elgin late
you tried to remember the colour
of her eyes all you could recall
was her hand on your forearm
the elbow swing the give of her
waist as you seesawed and wove
a ring and swung on through and
came back home

You broke her heart too dan—
the train doesnt run anymore
and if it did would it stop at
naperville? its long since
bob dylan went electric and poets
had three names now my beard
is as white as theirs and i
havent heard your voice for
a long time and still i honour
you in my mind where we sashay
back on home

SAYING GRACE

for Jim Cooney

The dank air in the greenhouse
held its breath

The stretched plastic shivered
like pale silk in the early sun

Everything was ready to grow

And that was when we had the
late storm and i finally knew
you werent coming back

You had gone leaving me
to tell the story

I never knew there was
a story to tell

2

Thirst is a word hard to say —
comes out hoarse and parched

Now sitting in my kitchen
i look at two apples in
a bowl and a glass of wine
red as the apples

Outside dark branches crack
on themselves to let ice crusts
fall to the snow

Yesterday i made bread kneading
harsh rye and cracked wheat into
mild white flour thinking *blend*
in tough

Annual tree rings have grown
around the thought of you
deep in the hard wood

3

Thirst i say to the icy trees
and the bowl of fruit

It is early spring and new
storm sewer pipes are angled
on the roadside waiting for
heavy equipment

Sirens far off come closer
and i think of my children

What can i tell my children
or all those i love?

Nothing is good enough for them

4

There is no story to tell
but i will say this for you:

I will say grace over this
bread and fruit and wine

Quench i will say and deep
inside me something breaks
and begins again

SOLSTICE

You were singing the words
sleep unlock loosen--
words so full of blood
and heavy in my hands
I carried them outside and
set them free rising to the
thin bush shy birds going up

Now our shovels are finding
the ground hiding under snow
our shovels strike fire from
the sidewalks stone and I
look up towards the trees

Last night the dark bandaged
their eyes now tall clouds
stride across the house

Now I want something to take
me up in its arms and say
what your hands are singing

TWO RIVERS

All day the sun on the leaves
the weather gentles the air --
a day of music in a high pure
light

Late bees drunk on the windfalls
striking the bright air singing

I am swimming in the naked air
like a man at one with the water
over pebbles bunched on the
rivers bed   riding the singing air
out to the place where it widens
to sea

You are probably walking down near
some river your fists in your pockets
hunched against it all thinking of
the sludge building up under the bridge
all those confused walking-by-water
thoughts and you observe the gulls and
barges think *hes not here with me* and
the river opens like a fist becoming
a hand

FOR MARGARET

I wake to the dark and
stare at my dream going
up through the roof and
look for the rooms stretched
walls my eyes could not
follow

You are deep in your own
dream in a place I can
never come to

Now my eyes are friendly
with the dark   the walls
are there again as usual
and I can just make out
the known shape of your
face so near to me closer
than my own or my dream

I sink back into dark
and dream of a country
where I am wholly known
the way you know me
in the noon of common day

DRIVING AT NIGHT

its a serious movie—
the road i mean coming
into your light before
you have time to say
the name of the place:
kankakee: *wabash: home:*

so this world always
comes at you and you
never touch it you are

alone with yourself and
those bodiless voices on
the radio like the road
and space sits on you
like a bully who wont
get off wont get off
it says there you go
there you go

RODRIGO: CONCIERTO DE ARUNJUEZ

As a diver on the edge gathers all his forces in, uncoils and is launched higher than he can reach, tries for the top of the air, then falls in a poised gesture of acceptance to the falling and the water, the music allows no extra gesture. It is a pain that enters itself, fills itself up so that there is no room for anything else. A face which has never seen a mirror says something so simple you forget to listen. Then you say *what* but it has passed will not speak again. A pain turned in on itself, a dry ache, no tears, words which can not be said, a music that hurts.

MY FATHERS WATCH

it has been silent in the drawer
since 1958 and i have to move it
when im looking for change and now
i lift it up into the rooms light

I rub a finger over the engraved name
my name the words *faithful* and *twenty
five* useless useless useless no hands

the crystal broke in the drawer in
1968 the hands are gone the spring
broken its useless

i put it back among the pens that dont
write the ticket stubs the odd screw
missing from something all useless

i put it back gently remembering me
on the bicycle down the alley my father
waiting by the gate   *hey*   i shout *dad
look no hands*

VISITING DAY

three years ago i started on midnights
now noon sun is nothing to me the clang
of a tireiron dropped on concrete
enters my dream of animals   possibly
wild dogs sniffing at my grave and in
the dream my father is ascending a hill
i am waiting at the top for him now
as the clang dies in the light and heat
i sit on the edge of the bed   my wife
brings me the mail   only a letter from
a friend saying *write when you get time*

father   i waited for you at the top
of my time watching your slow going up
how patiently you came on   *when are we
going home* i called down to you and
my words fell to meet you and you looked
up and smiled waving   called an answer
i couldnt hear   you smile and wave and call

father   what did you tell me

did you tell me of another hill
and other times for ascending

only this letter   *when you get time*

wild dogs race in the night fields

NEAR THE CROSSING

We dreamed the creosote smell
of long distance

Stood among tall weeds in the ditch

Heard the cicada summon summer

Loitered waiting for the train
to pass

Saw ourselves thick with purpose
looking out the diner window
at boys watching

Thundering steel on steel
answering the cicada

Leaving boys standing tall in weeds
smelling creosote in after silence
dreaming of distance waiting

NO SEASONS DIFFERENCE

I am a man looking down
a path shading my eyes
with my hand the sun tries
to pry under my hand I want
everything to stop this long
fall this never ending autumn
all the birds gone crazy the
leaves hanging on hanging on

I was coming down from the
high country of sleep the
house was heavy with sleep
I turned to say this in your
ear the gold in your ear you
carry like a small perfect
word I said there are no crimes

I said it is only a case of
long division birds began to
derange the day the morning
birds tear it all apart I
rise to say there are no
crimes I am looking down
a path it is burning with
light I am looking for
something to rush into my
arms I am waiting for winter

THE HOUSATONIC AT STOCKBRIDGE

for Charles Ives

You made me yearn for places Ive never been:
camp meetings   hymns at dusk   a river brown
as ale pouring itself over stones I cannot
touch

You took me to that place where the river
bends like an elbow leaning on a trains
window ledge

I thought of trains in the night passing
and a baseball glove hung up curling
to hold the hollowspace where the ball
is slung

I became a man in a straw boater walking
beside that river   a woman on my arm shy
and fervent bending her face away from
the words I said

You hold me in that hollowed space
like shaking air

LOGOS

I stood in the empty silo
looking up at the propped
open door a patch of sky
an unblinking blue eye
like a hole in the world
the end of the tunnel turned
on end and I said my name
to it echoed sounding up

It must have been like that
for god once saying his name
in the hollow silence looking
at his own eye seeing the
blue world serene unfold

FROM FAR AND NEAR

From far off they are coming down
the bridge going into lower gear
snow all over the tires the mud
guards flapping hung tired old wings.

At night they drive right into my
dreams coming home to a truck stop--
the one you have seen in kalamazoo
or east moline or in your dreams.

And the late ships under the bridge
salute each other deep and echoing
god! when I hear them I get weak
thinking of far off ports going
away so I lie still waiting to be
taken

Away but the bed is crowded with
all my dead sleeping uneasy and I
turn to stare through the wall into
winter dark remember walking out
past ideal auto sales light on the
windows of ed the workingmans friend
saying summer come from far come near.

RUNNING RIVERS OF MY YOUTH
RUNNING RIVERS RUN

I

Out beyond the limits of my eye
the river came to me came and
went on past me intent in its
going towards what I did not
know running past my eyes limit

Stooping I put my hand down
to touch the sand bottom felt
the waters urgent pull knew the
strange touch of far travelled
water

I learned to say it fingered
on a map learned said its name
but the river did not know
its name

I have known rivers since

The other rivers gave me far
places theyd been to and gone
those rivers at night running
secret and patient

Listen:
des plaines fox sangamon

I say the names to the dark
names strong as grass bent
gullied by their passage

2

Always I go back to that first
river of no name when I had
no name standing on cut gully
bank the large stones half wet
half white bone in dry light
knowing them sacred knowing
the rivers rill furrowing the
high certain field sacred
before I knew a name for my
self knowing my self whole

Somewhere beyond my limits
snow melted fell pooled
rivulets furrowed it began
patient gathering mining
down the sacred thing began

3

When the river froze over
and I stood on the sway
watching the waters skin
craze under my feet I was
out of bounds

In spring the river called
the shadows together in the
high field gathered the
scattered dark and the ice
broke and stately moved
down past my eyes limit

Fox des plaines sangamon
gathering falling towards
sea

4

Once I stood in cold
shallows once I crossed
from rock to rock felt
the current coax and I
lay down in sunlit water
looked over the cut bank
at the high field

That field my mother rode
horses in the night the
barn burned and the wild
horses were driven out and
my mother rode them to the
river and across their manes
on fire

Listen once more:
the water clear as gods eye

My mother was a girl who
rode wild horses my father
was waiting in the city
they would meet in that
city I would wake in to
this world and wait for
rivers

5

Last night I woke to rain
thought of rain falling all
across my yard down my
street far across all down
the river falling into all
the rivers into that river
I named before I had a name

Thought of rocks split by
water the earth mined by rain
rushing falling water in the
dark as I lay listening to
that patient water fall and
I dreamed myself back rode
horses of fire back to the
first river

Listen again:
the water clear as gods
eye cut gully bank brown
casually said to me death
and forever far away close
to you closer than your
name